OURS

NEW CALIFORNIA POETRY

EDITED BY

Robert Hass
Calvin Bedient
Brenda Hillman
Forrest Gander

*For*, by Carol Snow

*Enola Gay*, by Mark Levine

*Selected Poems*, by Fanny Howe

*Sleeping with the Dictionary*, by Harryette Mullen

*Commons*, by Myung Mi Kim

*The Guns and Flags Project*, by Geoffrey G. O'Brien

*Gone*, by Fanny Howe

*Why / Why Not*, by Martha Ronk

*A Carnage in the Lovetrees*, by Richard Greenfield

*The Seventy Prepositions*, by Carol Snow

*Not Even Then*, by Brian Blanchfield

*Facts for Visitors*, by Srikanth Reddy

*Weather Eye Open*, by Sarah Gridley

*Subject*, by Laura Mullen

*This Connection of Everyone with Lungs*, by Juliana Spahr

*The Totality for Kids*, by Joshua Clover

*The Wilds*, by Mark Levine

*I Love Artists*, by Mei-mei Berssenbrugge

*Harm.*, by Steve Willard

*Green and Gray*, by Geoffrey G. O'Brien

*The Age of Huts (compleat)*, by Ron Silliman

*It's go in horizontal: Selected Poems, 1974 – 2006*, by Leslie Scalapino

*rimertown / an atlas*, by Laura Walker

*Ours*, by Cole Swensen

COLE SWENSEN

# Ours

UNIVERSITY OF CALIFORNIA PRESS   BERKELEY   LOS ANGELES   LONDON

NATIONAL
ENDOWMENT
FOR THE ARTS
A great nation
deserves great art.

This project is supported in part by an award
from the National Endowment for the Arts.

University of California Press, one of the most distinguished university
presses in the United States, enriches lives around the world by
advancing scholarship in the humanities, social sciences, and natural
sciences. Its activities are supported by the UC Press Foundation
and by philanthropic contributions from individuals and institutions.
For more information, visit www.ucpress.edu.

University of California Press
Berkeley and Los Angeles, California

University of California Press, Ltd.
London, England

Designer: Nola Burger
Text: 8.25/13 Interstate Light
Display: Interstate, Deepdene
Compositor: BookMatters, Berkeley
Printer and binder: Friesens Corporation

Library of Congress Cataloging-in-Publication Data

Swensen, Cole.
  Ours / Cole Swensen.
    p. cm. – (New California poetry ; 24)
  ISBN 978-0-520-25463-3 (alk. paper) – ISBN 978-0-520-25464-0
(pbk. : alk. paper)
    1. Gardens – Poetry. 2. Gardens, French – Poetry. 3. Le Nôtre, André,
1613 – 1700 – Poetry. I. Title.
  PS3569.W384097    2008
  811'.54 – dc22                              2007037342

Manufactured in Canada

17  16  15  14  13  12  11  10  09  08
  10  9  8  7  6  5  4  3  2  1

The paper used in this publication meets the minimum requirements
of ANSI / NISO Z39.48 – 1992 (R 1997) (*Permanence of Paper*).

# CONTENTS

# ACKNOWLEDGMENTS

Warmest thanks to the following journals in which some of these poems first appeared: *Arson, Bayou, 1913, The Colorado Review, Carnet de Route, The Denver Quarterly, Ecopoetics, The Harvard Review, Jubilat, Kiosk, The Laurel Review, The New Review, No,* and *Pool.* And warmest thanks to French translators Suzanne Doppelt and Omar Berrada, who translated parts of the Medici section, and to the review *Vacarme,* which published them, and to France Culture, which broadcast them.

"The Garden as a Letter" and "The Garden as a United of Measure" were published in the anthology *Under the Rock Umbrella: Contemporary American Poets from 1951–1977,* ed. William Walsh (Macon, GA: Mercer University Press, 2006).

And my warmest thanks to Shari DeGraw of Empyrean Press for her letterpress broadside of "The Medici: Catherine"; to Sarah Roberts of Wells College for her broadside of "The Garden as Extension" in an earlier version; and to Elka Weber of Small Press Distribution for her broadside of "Paradise" in an earlier version. The section "Versailles" was published as a chapbook by Martin Corless-Smith in his Free Poetry series.

And I'd like to thank the Creative Capital Foundation very much for its generous support and guidance for this project.

The quotation from Allen Weiss in the poem "A Garden of Numbers" is from his book *Mirrors of Infinity: The French Formal Garden and 17th-Century Metaphysics* (Princeton: Princeton Architectural Press, 1997). The line "The world is blue like an orange" is a translation of Paul Eluard's "La terre est bleue comme une orange."

André Le Nôtre (1613–1700) is often considered the father of the French formal garden. As the son and grandson of royal gardeners, he was born in the Tuileries and inherited a tradition already quite old. He took those traditions and adapted them to early Enlightenment thinking, incorporating contemporary mathematical and optical techniques, such as anamorphic perspective, to create gardens unprecedented in their appeal to both the eye and the mind.

Versailles is his best-known work, but he played a crucial role in many other gardens, including those at Chantilly, Saint-Cloud, Sceaux, the Tuileries, and Vaux-le-Vicomte. This last was his first major commission, and it remains famous both for its perfection and for the scandal incited when it was unveiled for the king and his court in the summer of 1661. It was so grand that it threw Louis XIV into a fit of jealousy and convinced him that its owner, Nicolas Fouquet, who was also his superintendent of finance, must have been embezzling. Fouquet was arrested a few weeks later and spent the rest of his long life in jail.

That story and others inform some of the following poems, but none of them is necessary, or even particularly helpful, for reading the poems themselves. Similarly, a few proper names are mentioned here and there, not for their historical significance, but rather to underscore their bearers' simultaneous roles as average people doing daily things, such as loving gardens.

André Le Nôtre lived a long and prosperous life. By the end of his career, he was consulted by royalty and aristocracy all over Europe, and his influence had spread even farther. And yet one of the things that is most remembered about him and most often repeated is that he was a great guy – modest, fun-loving, easy-going, and friendly – so somehow it seems fitting that, although he created all his gardens for members of the most exclusive classes, they are today almost all public parks. As if to underscore the irony, the phrase "le nôtre" means "ours."

# A GARDEN IS A START

Because the kings of France loved Tivoli
                          these windows bearing oranges
                                                  globed,
glowed, and that's how night becomes day without taking your eyes off their palaces in winter.

A garden is a mirror
                  he said stepping back to get a larger view
                                          he knew
a globe upon a table, that's containable,
                          whereas an orange will seem to expand in the dark – we've trained
our explosions to slow down. We thought
the world was warm, was orange, and hung
                          ripe among the leaves all around us.
From the French:
*garder:* to keep as well as to tend: *gardien,*
*garde bien,* keep well, guard them
within
the horizon, stepping back, dropping off –
                                  here,
                                  he opens his arms, spreads out his hands, now off the map
"You will see

A garden is a window: A garden starts, of course, in the eye, which is looking out a window, which starts geometry on its rounds, each pane

                                    recording the faceted plantings

                                                      that a single finger traces

in the crisp veil of late frost,
some fortunes turn dust to dust.

André Le Nôtre spent his childhood among the gardens of the king and his gardeners studying to be a painter who paints "This lives"

who paces trees

who sees:

André Le Nôtre spent his childhood.

Everything he ever planted now is dead.

André Le Nôtre died a rich man.

*"Le Nôtre couldn't stand views that end" – Saint-Simon*

Half a century earlier, his grandfather had undertaken, on his own and at his own expense, to replace all the dead trees in the Jardin des Tuileries.

We
who were born in 1613
are we who remain
here in the garden as it leads outward
an owl of all edging
and compass inciting
obeisance and trust us –
we left for the forest
down a grand avenue of oaks
all leaning inward, they
leaned over as we spoke:
four rows of elm
all bordered in hawthorn
four huge coffers
of shadow in flower
for four kilometers of one
can only hope
for a good handful
of the restless
coming down to earth.

And to you we leave these trees.

To the elementary curve,

he said, the earth

and it turned
                    as things turn to stone with a word spoken
at a given angle to the wind.
You measure the angle with an astrolabe and needle,
                                        the needle balanced
                            on the middle finger and the eye aligned
to the eye          around which it glides.

He dreamed of a spherical garden
and listened to the spring tighten
as he wound the clock

counting slowly
as it slowly, unknowing, comes into view
reciting
        But I'm an astronomer,
I lose things.

# PARADISE

Certain traditions claim that man and garden cannot be separated,
or if and when they are, will neither still be visible, the inverse

of those twins that you never see in the same place at the same time. We disappear
through a single door, unrecognized

in the morning in the park, where we sit behind the early paper
and periodically declare I can't believe

in the Middle Ages, they drew the news on cemetery walls. A long line
of bodies in silhouette that swayed. This too, they say,

is paradise because the sky touches the ground wherever the former has a hole in it called a hand,
espalliered mansions and guests in the millions.

The first public gardens in history were called *oubliettes*. As soon as you entered,
you were indistinguishable from the animals.

## LEAVING THE MIDDLE AGES

When within walls:
    In the *Roman de la Rose,* the walls rose
There's a flower in the wall
     that falls out when the wall flowers
This is a Renaissance
    missing from thirst –
The garden fell apart, fell over, fell out
      into the world, making the history of gardens
the history of views. Principal tool:
     You sit on the terrace
until the world is a spindle,
     a woman facing west, and in her lap
two hands that run out of themselves, overhead,
the splayed magnolia blossoms
     and beyond them, their trees.
We are impoverished precisely to the degree
      that the garden will walk back in,
and the walls will rise again your arms are full
      and someone gets up to open the door
of bees.

# THE BIRTH OF LANDSCAPE ARCHITECTURE

The structure of many plants follows
that of the golden section:
                              width over length, length over width
minus the length
                    of a spiral stair
                              of leaf by leaf, between gravity and sun,
strung. All you have to do is enlarge it, make it the size of an average life, which lets it live twice.

Seventeenth-century gardeners
                              were trained in drawing, astronomy, cartography,
and geometry, which included the science of alignment,
all those intricate wheels
                    hand a boy a tiny engine – here, Montaigne sent this
from the gardens of the Villa d'Este,
                              where in the 1570s he saw fountains that triggered
organs and trumpets and the birds fell silent in swirls
                              through which he freely
                                        returned with Italy opening
a small mechanical heart in everything green.

# THE GARDEN AS ARCHITECTURE ITSELF

Much early landscape vocabulary was an attempt to make the entire world your home. Le Nôtre, in particular, saw a hallway in his walking and so walked into a clearing called "Festival Hall" or "The Water Theater" or "The Corridor of Mirrors," which multiplied the admission that only naming could bring this vast expanse
circling in, a chance ride in rings
kept in atoms
kept in jars on windowsills
                        who also had names beginning with
My other house is larger.

# THE GARDEN AS WORD GAME

And so a whole language developed
to say
        green matters and water,
no small part of any traveler,
                        came to be its own ceiling
spoken, always building:
                *parquet pond*
and gate beyond
                the *boulingrin*,
*parement*, and *vertugadin*, and then another gate
flagrant and beyond
                        which
                        with the exception of statues
which have no way of ending
                            in a stairway of celebrated shadow:
draft of flower
cousin of lawn. And we'll build you
while crossing
                a falling trellis
and we'll build you an alphabet
the leaves will orbit.

## THE GARDEN AS EXTENSION

Bronze horses round the bend of water.

La famille de Le Nôtre,
gardeners all the way back to the Fall,
                                        crowned a fountain
with intersecting shadows, the tip of the raised sword
just grazing that of the palm tree in summer
which makes it summer.

Who was born in a garden
                        We keep on coming forward
                                        If you think of the trees

as people. We were promised
                        *and Mary reached out to the gardener*
that from the poverty of touch
                        *who took a step back*
                                        And someday all this

has been said
by so many so often
that the voice becomes a park.

Does the verdant ever intersect the human?
Does the heart, that green thing stranded in an ocean.

He noted:

      *windy today, small gusts of rain*

"à partir de mes parterres"

              He laid out his gardens

                        in terms of tribes

                   that wandered as he turned and spoke

              to someone he can no longer see

in the doorway, which is like a land bridge

made of air.

       André Le Nôtre

                   was born in a difficult year. They spoke in numbers

and planted the seed of doubt at the heart of a flickering fruit, in this case, a pear

sliced open to its white flower without creases in a seedless center where shadow

becomes the point of the picture. Any garden is a description

of its era's metaphysics.

## SIR MINE

Come 1675. Come a home into a spine: To say "You are enobled,
Sir, you are

        a condensation of huge portions of the population and responsible
for their every whim. For instance, this blade of grass; the parallel is obvious – the king looked out
on someone else's expanse.

In 1675, Louis XIV made André Le Nôtre a noble. Who took three snails and a cabbage
for his coat of arms. Who is walking in my garden. Who is my garden
is also this vagrant, who upon waking would trace on the frosted window
a perfect copy of a landscape by Corot and within it, for just a minute, disappear.

## GARDENS BELONG

to the class of all things that go beyond.

Every garden is a rearrangement of a previous garden.

André Le Nôtre gardened like he was opening an envelope,
unfurling each arpent into what will,
                                    in a time-lapse film,
appear choreographed into its own life, a private ideogram
of land that would become increasingly public in spite of them.

# PRINCIPLES

. . . . . . .

## IN AN EFFORT TO MAKE THE GARDEN A STANDING PROOF

of the ascendency of reason over nature, strict rules governed its layout:
        the principal north-south axis must start at the back door
        and head straight toward
        an illusion of infinity intersected by perpendiculars that divide all space into near
            and thus

the chateau is set, a little jewel in a park, and the garden,
                        a little halt in the nerve. A little
unlikely order arcing through a forest always just
                   about to pour over the wall,
which makes the house fuse and the clouds adhere,
                 leaf by leaf
                     to the painted world
on a porcelain cup, an emerald castle, peridot trees

radiate from the center, a moth-white deer, terraced and made to float
above all
      *Close the door*
a corridor
      facets its way through stone; *house my diamond*
which writes on glass: *pass*
*by my window.* In which a boy sits looking out
both from and at an enormous forest.

## CERTAIN PRINCIPLES MUST BE OBSERVED

The initial impression must be from a height, but only half
that which is gained from the opposite extremity, looking back.

He watched the house, the courtiers coming in and out. The degree of the bow
measured. The king and his glances, a person

forsaken, once flayed itself upon a blade of grass.

                                     Such was the etiquette

that sharpened needles by accident,

                      a precision glittered

with the proper tools, which include:

                       Rules:

                          No trees

shall be planted within the *première vue,*

                              only low *parterres* and a few *arbustes*

cut close. So that every prospect is a little aerial; we plane above
a cloisonné; we lose track

of the conversation for a moment, and then snap back:

          a garden is a sequence that has no basis in fact:

                                     at the aura

                                     at the aurore

                                   at the slightest sound, corona;

it's a way of making nature account for the mind.

## A GARDEN OCCURS IN FOUR STAGES

with the house being first and the forest last, and in between
   1) the parterres, which suggest the inveterate, these violets
      and line effects and carved up things in plain sight
      of
   2) the bosquet, a nosegay made of 50-foot oaks, progressively lost,
a child placed a shell on a stone
and watched her home recede at the speed of light.

Way down there, the fine ladies walk
at a pace that makes
topiary make sense.

She said, I was playing a game
that involved pebbles and sand when the horses
bolted in the lane.

I lost a bet with the gardener's son—every one of them
lame. I arrange
my fingers in a square or in a series of squares
that each square fits within. I'll win.

## A GARDEN AS A LETTER

engraved an opening,
                              and so you open it, step by step, defined as that
intermediary point between darkness and diction. To write *I said it*
is already distant.
                         She would have used a *nom de guerre,* encoded
the time and place of the assignation. *I will see you*

walking down a long alley of overhanging trees.
I will see you from the back.

Le Nôtre tried
to make every alley extend endlessly into its final leap. In the letter
hidden in the book left in the grove as if forgotten
is an extension of diplomacy by other means.


      . . . .


The 17th century saw a curious rapprochement between gardens and war – fortifications were less interested in going up, where they stood as clear targets for recently evolved artillery, than they were in going out, in covering sufficient land to raise the crops to survive a siege. Thus the landscaping of war, and of holes within wars, where the living lived, and the view from the ramparts was good. Le Nôtre's wife, Françoise Langlois, was the daughter of a member of the French Artillery Council. She'd grown up in a walled garden, through which the world fell. And in the middle of it, there was a well.

## A GARDEN AS BETWEEN

as the articulating tissue between city and ocean, between building and
barren, around a house, a jungle
extends
       a magnet toward a jungle. A match
struck, a tailored knuckle; make it
              useful. Let it reign
              between the stilted and the flaming, the crack
in the glaze that lets us flow out again across a plain. A garden marks that plain
with a first principle. It paces off precise and hovers, cartilage between road and
home, a mental stable of dressage roses
                hovers
                as a garden is rooted
half in idea, rending the earth unstable, a flying machine with three wings, then
five, then all over the sky, in miniature vistas, a garden
branches from a fist in bridges.

## A GARDEN AS A UNIT OF MEASURE

They adopted the tools of the sea,
the astrolabe
            as if the island never came
became the graphometre of Philippe Danfrie, 1597,
                        which allowed a line
in the mind to falter on a sum
                and become a mile.
                And aid in pacing
                more precisely
                the edge cannot retain.
Gardens lie beyond the eye.

                The rest is a long walk
                toward a ship in flames.

# ANAMORPHOSIS

According to angle and alignment, the garden owns it, and the eye
gardens down the eye, sliding. The observer is a precise spot that a human sometimes enters.

. . . .

A garden is always seen
from an extreme angle.
This is because we are not very tall
                                        compared to the world,
which runs in breadth
                    way out ahead
                                    of the vertiginous
thousands
            will remain
                        and even neck to neck
will disalign. Stand here.
See that distant distance?
                            Stand there. There's a way to compute
the angle of incidence
                        says Euclid's eighth theorem
to reel in the world
                        we need a single viewer, said the view, who
said the person who never left the back door,
                                            who is still standing there in the doorframe:
I see a world so precisely distorted that I sit on the terrace
sipping champagne with a friend, and as the lights come on, the painting grows
within the trees and is the trees and if all of this fits within.

Le Nôtre used anamorphosis to make the world come home. Sad cataract
in a music box, there is no animal
that cannot learn.

## EUCLID'S EIGHTH THEOREM

says that identical parallel objects placed at different distances
from the eye are not seen in proportion to their distances
which proves the field of vision to be spherical
like trees that, though identical, move at different speeds
and all the paths
that started out infinitely curved
                                 roll slowly
across a space full of birds until the forest slows down so much
that a man can carefully plan
to place the body equidistant;
                             the body in the middle
which is his
           will wait
                  until the power of want ignites the tops of the trees in a line,
one by one, even a whim
will prove the Renaissance wrong:
                         it is not a flat plane hung before the painter's eye
like a window, but a glass float from a Japanese fishing net
that made it all the way across the ocean on a single storm, which places the world
among its objects, causing crossroads,
                            which is another mode of locating the body
as a series that necessitates a love of time.

# BECAUSE A GARDEN MUST END

Le Nôtre ended the world
in a *saut-de-loup,* which is to place a savage beast in the central path;
a cross-section in a corner of the blueprint
shows it clearly — he's mid-air in an arc
under which the children run laughing
                                in through the french windows
where they disappear like glass in water in another answer
                                        it's a dry moat
that keeps the world at bay while the line of sight continues unhindered,
both time and frame
                    arrayed along an elegance that rides a soft wolf
just above the ground.
Topire me a sky; shape it like a mind.

# IF A GARDEN OF NUMBERS

If a garden is the world counted
                and found analogue in nature
One does not become two by ever ending
                    so the stairs must be uneven in number
and not exceed
thirteen without a pause
of two paces' width, which
             for instance, the golden section
        mitigates between abandon
and an orchestra just behind those trees,
gradations of green that take a stethoscope: we risk:
Length over width
         to make the horizon run straight
equals
     to make the pond an oval:
             Width
             over length minus the width
       in which descending circles curl
into animals exact as a remainder.

       Which means excess. The meaning of the real
always exceeds that of the ideal, said someone.
                  He was speaking of Vaux-le-Vicomte,
but it's equally true of parking, or hunting, or wishing you could take it back. He

       who is Allen Weiss, actually said, "The meaning
of a plastic or pictorial construct always surpasses the ideal meaning of that work."
Which is something else entirely. Said
the axonometric
divided by
the anamorphic.
       There is nothing that controls our thoughts
more than what we think we see,
which we label "we."

# FURTHER NOTES ON THE COLLUSION OF TIME AND SPACE

Every point in space aims for an equally precise one in time. For centuries, Vaux-le-Vicomte
had been heading toward August 17, 1661, 6 pm: The carriages arrived.

                                     It's an elaborate exercise

in the distortion of perspective. We stepped out onto the back terrace,
and there it was, perfectly

                       sun
                       when suddenly

                                  a Grand Canal appeared and its swans, and its boats

in the shape of swans. There's a way to trace a path
so that from the terrace it looks continuous
though it's actually broken in several places by bodies of water, stretches of lawn
with occasional flowers that erase the air in gusts

                                into all that is not garden

is dance hall and ballroom

                    whose oval

                            circles as one approaches

women spring from carriages in ostrich feathers and competition
glitters,
slopes. It was the biggest fête they'd ever seen. Three weeks later,
Louis XIV arrested Fouquet,

                       for whom an ocean

continued to open
what he came to think of as someone else.

## WORKING CONDITIONS

The estate of Vaux-le-Vicomte was produced by three men — Louis Le Vau, the architect,
Charles Le Brun, the painter, and André Le Nôtre, who did the gardens. Wind and rain

start to work upon the margins          who brought three fingers
home in separate wagers                 as if they knew each other, three brothers
stood on a pier                         and the first brother said
(this is a joke)                        (and I quote)
                                        *The most distant parts of planes situated below the eye appear*
*to be the most elevated.* (Euclid's *Optics,*
tenth theorem) According to contemporary accounts, they were friends for life.

## CHARLES LE BRUN (1619-1690)

studied faces. He wrote the *Conference on the Expression of the Passions* in 1668
to explain how still the successful courtier must become, not a flinch
in the iris
        which tags us, not a vestige will cross the surface

                      except in a garden
          which is itself a face displaced

is a moment at the reflecting pool
               where, looking down, you could afford
to be moved. They'd show up in droves all alone.

Like Descartes, Le Brun believed that the spirit was corporeal and made the face
a glaze
     because physiognomy has become a precise science,
and only utter tranquility
          (The perfect courtesan had the look of porcelain.)
expresses the unity emblematic of this reign.

In 1988, Jean-Jacques Courtine and Claudine Haroche wrote a *History of the Face*. Of how
it gets used by people outside it. Le Brun's impassive faces were called the "zero degree of rhetoric"
because he was the interior decorator, making more and more inside, and not the gardener,
who hid his face in his hands and went on traveling.

## WATER

Early in mirrors

and into mirror, enter layer. An oar,
aviate in profile, we draw across the surface

all the mechanics. How the boat reaches
the tops of the trees, and so on

                    carved a sound. And yet we heard nothing coming.
Delible prow. Age
planed to castle shape, kingless
as we say in Spain,
               bell and swallow – each the echo
that makes the other
                the entire length of the canal
was used to tell fortunes. They'd keep it up for hours.
                            Anyone you know? No. And the other
whose fan made the world swing in its tiny frame: *Just perfect for your tiny hand, Madame.* No,
I had something else in mind.

## LABYRINTHS AND MAZES

And sometimes you're the door.

Within the stone

is a little maze: Make a list. Make each one different
shades of green and

a certain configuration of bones that ache
is a labyrinth that is,
said Madame de Sévigné, Fouquet's soul

for instance, the man has a garden for a body
and all his organs—the heart topiaried, and the *escalier d'eau*
of the spine.
                    One wonders if Fouquet really had either
she said or neither or *history is paltry* he was singing
                                             one night in the kitchen, as
rummaging about for a midnight snack,
he glanced out the pantry window
into the vegetable patch. Which spiraled, length over width, width over length
minus the width. Planets
are etymologically related to the plants that divide themselves
into carefully proportioned moments when
he turned around to find the kitchen maid staring,
"Monsieur,
                it is dark and entire
orchards are moving
                    in the perfect patterns of the quadrille."
Fouquet
followed her gaze, saying, "My
soul is a labyrinth. Madame de Sévigné has said so, and it makes me sad."

# OTHER GARDENS

. . . . . . .

## SAINT-GERMAIN-EN-LAYE

In 1122, Louis VI le Gros had a castle built on the Plateau de Laye for the view
and the wind.

And people are those little things way over there in red.

. . . .

A gardener's job is to open space
and not
to deal with mass.
And only rarely with color in a universe of green and sand,
a garden includes
everything you can see from the garden, so Saint-Germain-en-Laye
stretches far beyond Paris.

. . . .

When Le Nôtre replaced the gardens

When the superintendent of waters and fountains

When François Francine

complained that Le Nôtre showed no respect for resources.
Enormous poplars
and every ancient exchange of molecules. In gardening a representational art?

And he who is consumed by want

will fall asleep

counting. To everyone, there is one

impossible land. The endless lawn

appears as a straight line. The pain of singular time, as a tree must feel about space.

## CHANTILLY

The Prince de Condé every morning sent his horses

As Le Nôtre put it:
*Mon Sieur*    *never such*
              *an honor has*
              *and shall enslave*
              *myself, fountain and cascade*

And much later in a letter to the Count of Portland, Superintendent
of the Royal Gardens of England and Ambassador to France,
                                      he wrote,

"and above all Chantilly."

*Dear Kindness*
        *Dear Altesse*
                and endless
                      canal
                          to see such a river fall
                          in a single eye, such
                    terrasse

was there young again among paths.

                    *And I your servant*

                          *and I your calipers*

made them winners. From which windows, the clouds – that one, for instance,
the atomic structure of acres
                and that one, a thoroughbred racer in a dovecote.
And your stables full of ravens. We will,
                all our hats upon
                    this sunny day, capsize

in a storm
and with a horse under each arm, Madame, have you
the interlocking nature of even the smallest particles? Neck and neck
around the final curve,

it's so odd how horses in a dead gallop will nonetheless at each step bend their forward ankle slightly upward
in a gesture so delicate that a teacup becomes a lampshade, and the lamp, a coral reef.

# SAINT-CLOUD

If the ghosts lose
               who remembers on fire 13 October 1870 at the end of a forest

an ancient distance, in which Catherine de Medici is still winding her way over the Alps.

Bought by her banker in the late 1500s, a mere village, who took an aster each afternoon
and scratched in the lacquer "Here lies" aloft

a sister city, an outskirts by Atget, photographed, 1924.
                                  Pale in shelter
the eyes have their houses, incised, and to everything,
                                  its lightning rod and watershed,
its parapet in rank advance. The king was invited to dine
and the king died.


    . . . .


Which wandered from duchy to holy which worship
                           which body as skidding
transparent through timing, grew a center much greater
and the fifteen fountains
                  of Sanctus Clodoaldus, whose miracles still walk abroad
are now walking. Oh history of shudders, a series of sightings in daylight.


    . . . .


It was Henri III

who shocked in a  mirror

ran into a man
on the end of a knife, and it was here that the Comte de Sancerre
began his long travels backward
                    because a saint somewhere
left a rollerskate on the stairs

....

Here where Napoleon Bonaparte
staged his coup d'état
in an orangerie that Napoleon III destroyed some fifty years later

to gain a view of several miles, and in between

all these kings

who search their pockets

and look up asking

why am I dying

## MEUDON

There's nothing left.
                           He barely had time
to admire, they say,
                       recent restorations have shown
vandals and war
                   backing up toward the door
and the drive a half a mile long, along
the cities gallop in,
                    there's a city at the door
where there used to be a war
                             for here history can be refused; Le Nôtre did
for instance say
                The pavilions will never be finished
and of my stations
and stepped off the train

# THE MEDICIS

.......

# CATHERINE (1519-1589)

Catherine de Me
                    with her eye on the sea
                                    ordered a home in the Tuileries
so that her front door toward the Louvre
was balanced by a side door on the river (its galleries
come to it naturally) we search through its arches, as much ocean as palace,
and as you pronounce it: learning the word for arcade gave her nightmares
in which she learned to swim, and all over her hands
birds and flowering trees
                        see
                            petals, feathers, hibiscus,
                                            at the time was just a myth
that turned into a quarter of the world's vermilion. Catherine
de Thy
house must be falling
into the river; though she never got there, she kept on repeating

To escape. Graphite, perspective, and just a little vindictive. The land is woven into diminishing galleries
of whatever will flower sunlessly. She was a pacer
and required
miles and miles of overhanging trees.

She planned it in glass, a plane of splendor, a river driven into

                                        Where did you

build me this sullen altar. History favors

whatever lives. Catherine became obsessed with walking, and thought if she could only build

a vaster inner with a huge room just for weather. Paris had taken to setting itself on fire. She got used to it.

## MARIE (1573-1642)


Escaping the open
                   into an empty
                             haunted and left
her husband dead in the halls of the Louvre, mile after mile

began planting shrubs and a palisade across the river
                                         (Henri had a lover
she said
the palace in the air is coming closer. Sometimes it ceases to be
a necessary compromise between

and I see each leaf
hovering just beyond the window
                            the espaliered trees
keep me up at night.
One of many fountains
and its fleet. And here I place the queens of France every so many paces
and I pace.

In 1613, Marie de Medici ordered the construction of the Arcueil aqueduct to bring the waters of the Rungis to what was to be the Luxembourg Gardens. It was Thomas Francine, the Superintendent of Waters and Fountains, who oversaw the work. Aerial water, in its long walk into ether. Thirty-one meters of marble later, they added another forty-six. *Balustrade* as in *balader* as in *ballade*. To what are we not connected. Wondered Marie as she added a few more hectares.

Her life was a shambles. A husband with 56 mistresses and 17 children not particularly
liking children she literally went to war with her eldest son, who won.

She whose dowry was a million. Who thought in terms of kingdoms, the basic unit of exchange.

She was appalled at the rustic condition of the Louvre. And of the spaciousness of space.
Lined in grace, opened onto awe until it became

some inconvenient "now"

why not stay

on like stone. The third one to the left as you enter the Luxembourg Gardens from the Porte de Vanves,
between Laure de Noves and Marguerite d'Angoulême. Ten feet tall. In the next one, I get to be a hunter.

Walking out on the first day of summer, 2007, Marie
sees hundreds of people playing on the lawns and in the paths
which have been completely redrawn, and the green metal chairs,
their particular sound as they're dragged across gravel. And the green metal chairs
full of people quietly reading paperbacks and newspapers, who look up,
startled to see her.
                          She stood a full minute, shocked, and then started screaming.
The rue d'Assas has cut off the entire northwest sector, and half the trees are gone.
The other half have unconscionably grown.

It was a night so warm you could walk through it entirely naked. Marie tried it, marching out the back door with a defiant air. Too bad nothing ever actually happens in such cases – no ghosts, no lightning, one ends up sitting on a rock under a tree, thinking.

Everyone has one gesture or expression

that shows them outside of time,

which is to say, at whatever single second of their lives struck a precise equilibrium between mind and face (time and space). Some it hits at 21, some at 30, some at 10,

but it never completely leaves. For Marie, it was her scream. Several people looked up, but there was nothing they could do.

# THE LUXEMBOURG GARDENS

The gardens were first opened to the public by Mademoiselle de Montpensier in 1672. Some say. Others,
that it was Gaston d'Orléans some twenty years earlier, and still others, that a garden is, by definition, a crack
in the armature
                         of who defined the public
                                              was constructed
of otherwise missing limbs, remembering
that there is no difference between land and landscape
                                                   I carry my window with me
until
there is no difference.

Who walked into this garden? If you had walked into this garden
would you have recognized it as such? Would you have recognized yourself? Every garden
is a portrait

because Jacques Boyceau de la Barauderie (1560-1633) clearly stated
that it was only by learning portraiture,
by learning to paint the face,
that the face could train a gardener's apprentice into a taste for the beautiful
that would later turn arabesque
to ornament,
                    for its own part, imported
                                        (Simon Vouet and all his travels) I
did not travel. Nor was I allowed to enter the garden—I stood at its edge and watched it unravel
and waited
for it to arrive.

A garden is a tide.

A garden is a tithe.

# VERSAILLES THE UNFURLED

In this lost world
                    a king would prefer
to be elsewhere, so he built one.

          At their height, the gardens of Versailles
covered more than 6,000 hectares

                              whose movement is outward
will crown and survive it. Imagine
the sweeping hand that says "This

As early as the 11th century, there's a record of a village called Versaliae on this spot. Butchers, ironically enough, who survived in part because it lay along the route used to drive the sheep down from Normandy.
                    And two lakes
                    and a river running out of them called Versailles-a-val-de-Gallie.
There was a windmill where the Cour de Marbre now stands, and enough wind to make a horse and enough strife to feed him on. They razed the town

and drained the lakes, and then set about wondering where they'd get enough water for it all.

Early in his reign, Louis XIV became fanatical about water. How to run countless fountains, several ponds, and miles of canal? He employed engineer after engineer to detour the waters of various rivers into Versailles. Because all its bodies — ocean, river, fountain, basin, glass in your hand — compose a single communicating system, and all are linked to God. A reflection is His gaze. Of which Narcissus died. Pierre-Paul de Riquet suggested the Loire. That having failed, Louvois proposed the Eure; Arnold de Ville, the Seine. Armies of them.

And the fountains
          always started in a given order:
                    at les Couronnes,
                    at la Pyramide,
                    at l'Allée d'eau,
                    at the sight of a stranger, who
being 98% water and liable to mistake
its inordinate price for his own. Dismembered sun
                    at le Dosme,
                    at l'Apollon
                    at the feet of the horses, where all sovereigns are crowned,
Louis XIV remembered certain things, and made sure that no one else had any idea what they were.

The 17th century saw water as the perfect metaphor for life – even when still,
the muscle cocked, a cliff to come. No one was allowed
to touch the surface of the ponds.

                    And begin again:

                                at la Latone
                                at les Aigrettes
                                at les Bosquets

                    and so on

        at my heart of stone

at my tangible swarm

a man in a boat
is mistaken for one. And for a moment

What is he doing on my own! asks the king. Who refused to be alone
or even to speak if he wasn't in the mood.

at my severed hand

at my distant tooth.

To every sense, every possible end. He planned the sound
from a long way off

that one fountain would fade at the precise
edge of the next
hearing field. We smell water

exactly twenty-five feet before we see it
according to the average velocity
of wind and its direction said Le Nôtre I am happy

to have here in my hand

the five senses
win 9 times out of 10

Thus a garden must also taste and touch. Thus water, which follows
natural law
          that all laws say "no more than it takes"
to prove
he held the water down by hand
so it wouldn't taste so much like steel.

As for the king, wherever he looked
the fountains played insatiably and the courtiers bowed despite themselves
and made the we who would believe
they'd say
it is not I
who would carve a separate country from the center of this man. Le Nôtre made the rounds
with him, and they argued about how to graft trees.

# THE DIVINITY OF THE SUN KING

Because they believed it, he built his private room

in the middle of the chateau, which sat in the middle of the park, which was planned to coincide with the exact center of the world physical, philosophical, and spiritual, and like his nested castles, the sign at the center of every seed is a sun; they're interchangeable, not because they're equal, but because they're identical. Louis XIV really believed he was light and had a lemon for a heart. The art of startled fountains, the lark nesting in harm.

## THE GARDEN AS A MAP OF LOUIS XIV

Is politic. And it's practical to have it
                                        rather calm. They talk of war
in avenues of trees. The trees inside the walls
are carved to points. The king points out
                                        and is proud to point to something that
        while not exactly moving, is undeniably alive. They've been talking
about the war for so long, there is no
commensurate
                constellation
                                or way to make a heel make
a sharp sound in sand. So how can you count

how many walked out, and how large is this room
they're walking through. Talk
is often pictured as transparent, for instance, in the drawings, whole armies
become avenues of chestnuts or limes.

# LE NÔTRE'S DRAWINGS

All history has founded its armies on the principle that when a shadow falls at a 45 degree angle, stand equidistant and think of the center of the earth, which has nothing of this world about it. Thus the extra arms. Look at Le Nôtre's plans, the rivulets and painted fans, the cypresses of silver.

And we sail away on a film of sun. Sun hitting a film of dust
across water makes it solid. In the drawings
well-dressed men stroll along canals adjusting their gloves. There are steel girders
that will later become invisible that hold certain flowering beds at just the height
to reach out and pick, and others, at eye-level, seem even more than usual
both right there and unattainable
sweet peas, strawberries, artichokes the size of helms. He drew them all in flower,
and they flowered.

## AND THE BIRDS, TOO

And the birds, too, a separate organ,
                          sweeping up,
                          a curve like a paper cut,
            a riot act
got rich in the trees.

They escorted the birds in carriages
                         drawn by swans.
                                    It's a long way from the station
crooned my aunt
                who made a fine chapeau of the pheasant her husband had
just shot. They called it a park.

Versailles, for instance

had any number of doors

which one will find when unannounced. There's a certain bow
handed down that evokes
swallow in a bosquet, owl all over town. Even today,
a cape afloat on a lake.

Anything numerous is therefore divisible, so
profligate this:
nightingale of ancestors who waterfall among the disappeared, an ear
on its own, ambient as sky
                         held up to the light
                                    there's a marble courtyard
in every act, a clearing, and you stumble upon

the decision to take this path, not that one. And will,
if you can,
send the other on home.

A garden is a machine
for multiplying
                   whatever you might have there in your hand – lines, veins, birds
in a more basic form.

A garden is an allergy

which is always a wish to place

a wish beyond the body. A clock is striking. Pierced, laced. Metallic taste. I'll wait.


Where an old woman can fall asleep

                            in a public park in July

a book in her hand and start up at a sound and then fall back to sleep again.

A garden is an asymptote, an infinite
approach, to touch your lip, something
slips
too close to I
watch the sky coming closer
and closer to your eye
and flinch.
        Louis XIV really believed
that the sun inhabited incidental things,
as if you could open a jar of sugar forever.

And the birds, too, a sense of touch, pavilion
in its chartered flight
                              that would precipitate
in slight crystal
or light broken through icing
                              will insect into wings

all over the flowers. Petals that act
                              the magnifying glass
that sets the place on fire from time to time
                                        a polished sun
                    will add
the theory that every grain of sand
that enters an eye. There stands paradise
in the way.

## THE REIGN OF LOUIS XIV

inaugurated a malleable earth, a thing
that could be turned over in the hand and made perfect, given time and unlimited weather.
It was an age that felt that nature could be corrected. More red. Less said. No flies. And
a few dozen rivers smoothing into numbers, any body of water

                                        turns slowly into a clock
                      and so it was not we

who arranged his hands

                            there were flowers on the table

she couldn't stop touching

                            white and overlapping

if you hold them you bruise

                            and to refuse

so that the hands remain on the table

                            and were arranged – the peony

as a crowd, clapping.

# THE GHOST OF MUCH LATER

There's a story that goes: On August 10, 1901,
two English schoolteachers walking in the gardens of Versailles took a wrong turn and found themselves back
in 1789 with the revolution just a day or so away. Full of gazebos and messengers, the whole scene was pretty
frantic, or else these two women, rather oddly dressed for the occasion, would have attracted more attention.
Marie Antoinette was sitting in the sun, reading in the backyard of the Petit Trianon. If it had happened to us,
we'd have been burned at the stake for our zippers alone. I have no idea how they got back, but they did, and
wrote a novel about it, and got themselves interrogated, etc. but never broke down.

Time can't move. Tattooed or engraved with a stylus: You
found a parterre in a newspaper, and thus we arrive at a future, but I've always thought

They could have proved it with a buried key, a canceled stamp, but
they could not. I've always thought
the saddest thing about ghosts and the only part
that's really frightening is just that *not*. Time
should not have frozen on a certain day in August
locked into a tree that opens on touch and we count the rings

and say "it saw the day"
                    Babylon hung
                           and Rome burned and Lisbon fell into the sea.

André Le Nôtre thought that by gardening along the strictest principles of geometry, time would come apart
in his hands. There goes private property.

Viewed from the chateau, the parterres,

                                                there are endless parterres,
the partners slide. There are precedents for such interchange, metal-
against-metal, the dust undisturbed, the dust arranged.

We arrange it in perfect sprays,
we rake
and comb. And some come undone. Some get lost.

Turning a corner – it's usually in turning a corner too fast – or in glancing back,
the length of each terrace is out of proportion to its width. And now farther.
Throws a stone and wherever it lands, she disappears – a disheveled woman
who didn't belong. With visitors all around. You try to ignore them,
but then suddenly declare, she had a birdcage on her head
and the birds said
what she would have said, had there been time.

Marie Antoinette was last seen reading, and she didn't look up. There wasn't a revolution going on. Or maybe sewing, there was something pinned together, she was holding something together, or whatever was ever in her hands that was several then broke into separate. Marie. Is by definition bordering the sacred, which is the universal, so it was no longer her garden. So she refused to raise her eyes and watch two middle class women have a right to these rooms in which they should have frozen to death in an instant. Instead, they dusted. They drew a gloved finger across a mantel and propagated hemophilia. All my children running down the drain. There have been fewer centuries than I have ancestors, and any one of them could blind you by glancing your way she said what do you mean "*nice*"? I am not this dust, I am not just once

floating downstairs in the sun. One woman heard her turn a page, while the other heard a leaf rattle across the terrace, and turned to watch it, more out of idleness than anything else.

# STATUARY

. . . . . . .

⋮

Anywhere that mineral here
would slowly grow, would there an air,
                              a little like a person
stands still a moment on the stairs, as would a person
refusing
            to change his address. If we take
the environment as a whole
                        and insert a statue of Massenet, or
one of Montaigne on which a pigeon builds a nest.
                                    They also live as doors, traced
                                    a portal to this world
and that among the blades where the shattered lawn, all a game
in which the pieces come together again. A statue makes
                                        a shore, a port, a storm.
                        The circle of philosophers
in stone; riven by voices, they stand at crossroads; they incite fountains. The voices
grow louder whenever someone lives.

If we take the environment as a whole, the function of statues is to cast shadows, and are in this respect the natural children of trees. In pallor, to palliate, to whiten, or to startle into light

shudders

a moonstone,
stone lantern,
alabaster lamp,
that the bone of a planet
would glow a little when mixed

a little

Apollo buried to the knee. Ulysses with a granite sail and whose granite wings? Across all night the rolling green, which does, at night, start up like a sea; you can hear it just beyond the gates, crashing on its hands.

They stand where placed, each face

                                  chosen for its cliff. A wind

in the leaves overhead

leaving a pattern of soft migration on the skin.

The silhouette of a man walking across the far terrace at Saint-Cloud is eclipsed for an instant
by a statue in the middle distance that it precisely fits.

Statues are a way for a king to be everywhere at once the body flung. There was
a time it rained gloves; another time, hands. They hold on. A king will turn
into history, and this is what it is to have a body
built of snow – lungs of snow and eyes and ice. From time to time,
Louis placed living men dressed as stone among his guests who would then
burst forth, as if he himself, my twenty fingers,
he said, my seventy, I am.

The statue as an intermediary stage between tree and man. Tree as intermediary between stone and sun. It was a language, and it spelled a name in space that erased space.

# ORANGERIES

. . . . . . .

⋮

By the light of oranges, strangers

bring the sea. Stack it here. Then quietly leave. Olivier de Serres

in 1600 suggested a return
to ancient methods — plant the trees in niches, open to the sun in summer and
glass them over in winter. Which are doorways
that open into stone. Oranges feel at home there, and lemons find a little light
shared.

The first orangerie in France was built in Amboise at the end of the 15th century,
but the form reached its height in the 17th
coinciding with what's called "The Little Ice Age,"
a series of exceptionally cold winters
                             of glass gathered, layered
rime on the arcing
                 arcaded sky. They built fires
in the basements and set the heat loose to run around in pipes. What possible
genetic advantage could there ever have been in dying of the cold?

So they invented the wheel

and rolled out the trees to sit in the sun like the invalids they weren't.
                                                              Orangeries

are built like stables –
                    winter light files
                                   pales
                                       itself in perfect order
                                                           prior
                                                           If a verger

is one who braids a leaf to navigation
is this green that never warms – Winter light is made of mica,
                          and as if magnetic, orbits
as it quietly devours
citrus flowers.

And so the trees were stabled

and breaking a window,

running in the sun, it swarmed spherical

which must be protected

by windows. There's something nicely tight in that. I like
a defiance that turns to you and says

make the sun touch
the very back
where the laurels and the pomegranates live.

The entire court rubbed their shoulders

                                        with the oil that misted from the folded peel

facing south

came to mean

        You'll never last.

A stretch of music chalked on a wall.

Colbert had 270 orange trees and arranged them all according to height, with the shortest closest,
so that it seemed
a thousand acres if you only reach
the shore by evening we will guarantee

and walked out the next morning
to find their order chaotic

which is not a tropical island
                    perched on a scissors' point – all my bahamas

are no less serial, we raise and lower them in time with the tides. *The world is blue*
*like an orange*
is true. The history of exotic fruits parallels that of the rising middle class, and spice, each
shared a fissure, then a fault
at the bottom
of what sea
          flowered a tree.

## "YOU ARE A HAPPY MAN, LE NÔTRE"
.......

– Louis XIV

# ON HAPPINESS

How can we say whether or not someone who lived from 1613 to 1700 was happy? Among the many things that make me want to go back in time is the incommensurability of vocabulary, particularly that involving feelings, but even all adverbs and adjectives — such as old, or scented, or slowly — even nouns float cell by cell into some other

say we planned it. Say I measured. Say this is a large city, and here is this very edge, and here this garden. Some say that Le Nôtre was first employed by Louis XIII's brother Gaston, who lived at the Luxembourg Palace, which was at the time more distant. It was miles away. It took us days to get there. While today, the power of his smile would slay us from the inside if we even tried it.

## PSYCHIC BOTANY

Le Nôtre was a happy man. Said the bio note on the back of his book, in the present tense, we say
I am
a man
who lost all three children in childhood
who had hidden inside them
a coiled childhood, the growth spiraling
there on the stairs for centuries
                              some philodendron
live for over a hundred years,
some pines, a couple thousand. I never planted pines, finding them too set
(he said) already in their conical shape. I wanted to shape them.

## THE GARDENED HEART

                        That Le Nôtre, known
for kindness and thought
                        to carefully turn
this selvage and torch
                you'd think a field
                                in flame
made of flames that would carry
                        a blue fruit entire
red anchor, now flower. He was a kind man
and that has lasted longer than everything
he ever grew from tower into tower.

## TUILERIES, JANUARY 2007

And to the mystery of private property
                              add five
centuries who in time
                    added time to the list,
                    a hazy distance
                    in a tiny enemy
of many.
Now they leave the Tuileries
open in winter until 7 pm. It's long past dark
and there are people scattered all through it
walking silent and alone and at home.

# KEEPING TRACK OF DISTANCE

Which is to walk
the scattered share
                        or pare it to a pilgrimage
arranged along an outstretched arm
pointing to the point of vanishing. How well the world
converges and just how well it counts,
for instance, Versailles
incorporates 13 miles of paths, which means we crossed a continent
every year or so in after-dinner strolls. It was always night there
with torches floating by in unmanned boats,
with boats of musicians passing in the dark
making their thoughts stand out
in the air. Arabesque.
                        Are of dome.
                        And freighters passing later on
with no lights
and no sound.
You might return
along an unknown road.